Strategic Studies Ins

ARMS CONTROL AND E

Stephen J. Blank
Louis H. Jordan, Jr.
Editors

August 2012

The views expressed in this report are those of the authors and do not necessarily reflect the official policy or position of the Department of the Army, the Department of Defense, or the U.S. Government. Authors of Strategic Studies Institute (SSI) publications enjoy full academic freedom, provided they do not disclose classified information, jeopardize operations security, or misrepresent official U.S. policy. Such academic freedom empowers them to offer new and sometimes controversial perspectives in the interest of furthering debate on key issues. This report is cleared for public release; distribution is unlimited.

*****

*****

Comments pertaining to this report are invited and should be forwarded to: Director, Strategic Studies Institute, U.S. Army War College, 47 Ashburn Drive, Carlisle, PA 17013-5010.

*****

All Strategic Studies Institute (SSI) publications may be downloaded free of charge from the SSI website. Hard copies of this report may also be obtained free of charge while supplies last by placing an order on the SSI website. SSI publications may be quoted or reprinted in part or in full with permission and appropriate credit given to the U.S. Army Strategic Studies Institute, U.S. Army War College, Carlisle Barracks, PA. Contact SSI by visiting our website at the following address: *www.StrategicStudiesInstitute.army.mil*.

*****

The Strategic Studies Institute publishes a monthly e-mail newsletter to update the national security community on the research of our analysts, recent and forthcoming publications, and upcoming conferences sponsored by the Institute. Each newsletter also provides a strategic commentary by one of our research analysts. If you are interested in receiving this newsletter, please subscribe on the SSI website at *www.StrategicStudiesInstitute.army.mil/newsletter/*.

ISBN 1-58487-545-3

CONTENTS

FOREWORD

While much attention is always given to issues of strategic and nuclear arms control, the conventional arms control agenda remains something of a step-child. Nonetheless, in regards to European security, conventional arms control issues are of the utmost significance. Indeed, since Russia suspended its observance of the Conventional Forces in Europe Treaty in 2007, there has already been one war in Europe, the Russo-Georgian war of 2008, and many subsequent rumors of war. Indeed, one could arguably claim that since that Russian suspension, progress on ensuring European security has stagnated, if not worse.

Bearing in mind the importance of these issues to European security in general and Russian ties with Europe and the United States in particular, as well as the connection between the conventional and nuclear arms control agendas, the Strategic Studies Institute (SSI) is pleased to present our readers with this monograph wherein three distinguished U.S., European, and Russian experts outline the parameters of these thorny interrelated issues. These papers represent the views presented at the SSI-Carnegie Council conference at Pocantico, NY, from June 1-3, 2011, and were subsequently revised for publication by the editors. Taken together, these articles fully clarify the multiple and complicated dimensions and connections linking these issues of conventional arms control and force reductions in Europe to the wider strategic and nuclear issues in which the parties are also involved. In this respect, they embody a major part of our activity in fostering international analysis and dialogue on topical security issues for the benefit and enlightenment of policymakers and experts.

At the same time, the presentation of these papers represents one more example of SSI's ability and willingness to partner with major think tanks and organizations devoted to the analysis of contemporary strategic issues, to bring international experts together in candid, high-level, and wide-ranging discussions, and to publish papers and books dealing with these issues for the benefit of our audience. In this spirit, we present these essays to our readers.

DOUGLAS C. LOVELACE, JR.
Director
Strategic Studies Institute

CHAPTER 1

THE PRECARIOUS AND FAR-REACHING CURRENT UNDECIDABILITY OF THE CONVENTIONAL FORCES IN EUROPE TREATY

Paul Schulte

BACKGROUND

Updated analysis of interests, possibilities, and implications for the ground-breaking Conventional Forces in Europe (CFE) Treaty is timely. This is less because the diplomatic situation of CFE itself has been observably changing (attempts to modernize it into a universally observed Adapted Conventional Forces in Europe [ACFE] Treaty remain in long-term stalemate), but because there are new arguments over how much it might be worth paying for its reanimation. While the future of the CFE project is certainly gloomy, it remains unresolved at present in Europe, though possibly replicable elsewhere.

HISTORICAL SIGNIFICANCE

In considering CFE's disputed future and wider significance, it is paradoxically helpful to look at the deeper past. There is an instructive contrast between the adaptation of the CFE Treaty with the complex and long-running 19th century Schleswig-Holstein Question. The perennial British Foreign Secretary John Henry Temple Palmerston said that "Only three people have ever really understood the Schleswig-Holstein business—the Prince Consort, who is dead—a German professor, who has gone mad—and

I, who have forgotten all about it." The group of specialist policymakers and academic commentators for CFE/ACFE often seems only slightly larger. Both the Schleswig-Holstein and CFE questions were not only famously complicated, but also largely incomprehensible to the public.

They also perfectly illustrate diametrically different approaches to military assertion and the role of armed force. The Schleswig-Holstein Question was built on dynastic convolutions and the complexities of feudal law. It was resolved violently. The Second Schleswig War of 1864, in which a rising, revisionist Prussia took the dominant military role, can be seen as a move from the concerted conservative stability of post-Napoleonic Europe into the cycle of 19th and 20th century nationalist and, later, ideological conflicts which tore Europe apart until 1945 and kept it separated until 1989.[1] The CFE project is an attempt to prevent further wars or military blackmail in the Eurasian continent stretching from the Atlantic to the Urals, by rigorously formulated obligations to provide military transparency, and legally enshrined controls on allowable holdings of key weapons.

During the early days of CFE, Robert Cooper, now Counsellor to the European External Action Service, even erected a theory[2] which framed and exalted CFE as the defining expression of global post-modernity, into which Europe would lead the world by seeking transparency and mutual trust rather than relying on balances of Westphalian national power, and threatened or actual resort to arms. "Intrusive verification—which is at the heart of the CFE system—is a key element in a post-modern order where state sovereignty is no longer seen as an absolute . . . [and] . . . security is based on transparency, mutual openness, interdependence, and mutual vulnerability."[3] The German Foreign Ministry, with its large arms control constituency, therefore characteristically tends to refer to CFE as *the capstone of European security*. They, like others, additionally point out that it is also a treaty that could be uniquely valuable in moving from codifying defense relations in the Cold War world into addressing post-Cold War arrangements where agreements have to be multilateral, there are no simplifying alliances and parity has no easy bipolar meaning.

This chapter's main predictive theoretical proposition is that in fact, progress on conventional arms control in Europe will continue to move at a pace dictated by nuclear atmospherics. This is because CFE, and, before it, mutual and balanced force reductions (MBFR), have expressed the wider state of East-West strategic relations, above all between the United States and Russia. These relations have been anchored on an overriding concern for nuclear stability.

NEGOTIATING HISTORIES

The historical record bears this out: The MBFR negotiations process was initiated as a result of U.S.-Russian détente, which culminated in an agreement between Richard Nixon and Leonid Brezhnev at the 1972 Strategic Arms Limitation Treaty (SALT) meeting to move forward by separate political and military negotiations.[4] The Conference on Security and Cooperation in Europe (CSCE) would deal with political negotiations and MBFR would deal with military issues.

Bloc to bloc MBFR negotiations began in Vienna, Austria, in October 1973 to reduce conventional military forces in Central Europe to equal but significantly lower levels. The talks were stultified by disagreements over Limitations on Residual Forces (how national sub-ceilings should apply after reductions), Associated Measures (the North Atlantic Treaty Organization [NATO] sought confidence building measures [CBMs] such as prior notification of maneuvers and acceptance of observers, while the Warsaw Pact rejected this as over intrusive and insisted that National Technical Measures should suffice), and the Data Discrepancy (how large the Warsaw Pact forces actually were). No substantive progress was made, although the process itself, despite its protracted frustrations, was judged by many to have been worthwhile in facilitating strategic dialogue between East and West.

But MBFR was ostentatiously stalled in 1979, as one of many angry Soviet responses to NATO's decision to deploy new intermediate-range nuclear weapons in Europe. After the intermediate-range nuclear forces (INF) crisis was surmounted, and the Cold War wound down, the MBFR talks were formally ended in 1989 and overtaken by negotiations in the new CFE framework.

CFE achieved a historically rapid movement to signature in 1989 between the two blocks[5] on tanks, armored combat vehicles (ACVs), heavy artillery, combat aircraft, and attack helicopters—the weaponry most important for large-scale offensive operations, collectively referred to as treaty-limited equipment (TLE). Thereafter, while the strategic atmosphere between Russia and the West remained benign, by the end of the Treaty's reduction period in 1995, the 30 States Parties completed and verified by inspection the destruction or conversion of over 52,000 battle tanks, ACVs, artillery pieces, combat aircraft, and attack helicopters. By the end of 1996, CFE states had also accepted and conducted more than 2,700 intrusive on-site inspections.

Subsequent events created the obvious imperative of adapting the Treaty to take account of the dissolution of the Warsaw Pact and the possibility of NATO expansion. For this, the key agreed features[6] were:

- *National Ceilings* on TLE that states can deploy within the treaty's area of application, which stretches from the Atlantic to the Urals (ATTU).
- *Territorial Ceilings* on TLE that can be deployed in each country within the ATTU.
- *Temporary Deployments*: requirements to notify additions to territorial ceilings for military exercises, temporary deployments or "exceptional circumstances."
- *Transparency*: a requirement on states parties to permit inspections of 20 percent of their "objects of verification," down to regimental level, and storage, repair, and reduction sites with TLE present. Annual or quarterly reports on the actual location of tanks, ACVs, and artillery were also required, together with notification of increases in a state party's holdings of combat aircraft or attack helicopters anywhere within the ATTU.
- *Flank Limitations*: CFE's biggest challenge had probably been Russia's discontent with treaty sub-ceilings imposed to prevent dangerous concentrations of TLE in the so-called northern and southern "flank" zones of the ATTU, adjacent to and including Norway and Turkey. But Russia remains the only state with treaty limitations on deployment of its own forces on its own territory, in the sensitive St. Petersburg and North Caucasus military districts. The 1996

review conference agreed numerical and geographical changes to the flank rules for Russia and Ukraine, with additional transparency measures to meet the concerns of other flank states.

The ACFE flank accord allowed new, higher limits on Russian battle tanks, ACVs, and heavy artillery deployed or stored in the now-reconfigured flank zone. According to President Bill Clinton in his Letter of Transmittal to the Senate of 1997:

> The Flank Document confirms the importance of subregional constraints on heavy military equipment. More specifically, it revalidates the idea, unique to CFE, of limits on the amount of equipment particular nations in the Treaty area can locate on certain portions of their own national territory.[7]

During the ratification process, there were congressional anxieties that Moscow might use the new rules to prolong an imposed presence in Georgia, Ukraine, Moldova, and Azerbaijan, together with fears that the Clinton administration would be too accommodating to this pressure in order to facilitate NATO expansion. Before giving its consent, the Senate consequently insisted upon additional assurances with regard to the sovereignty of the former Soviet republics.

The ACFE Treaty text was therefore signed at the Organization for Security and Co-operation in Europe (OSCE) Istanbul summit in November 1999 on the basis of Russian undertakings to withdraw from the Republic of Moldova, to reduce equipment levels in Georgia and agree with the Georgian authorities on the modalities and duration of the Russian forces stationed on Georgian territory, and to reduce their forces in the flanks to the agreed levels of the ACFE Treaty.[8]

But worsening disputes over NATO enlargement, and the intentions behind U.S. missile defense (MD) plans, eroded Russian willingness to comply with its Istanbul Commitments. Consequently only Belarus, Kazakhstan, Russia, and Ukraine ratified the ACFE, and Russia's ratification has been suspended.

In 2007, emphasising the unacceptability of "the extraordinary circumstance" of the introduction of U.S. missile defenses in Europe, President Vladimir Putin demanded a rewriting of the ACFE Treaty and warned of a moratorium on Russia's observation. NATO refused to change its policy, and Russia subsequently imposed the moratorium—almost certainly in legal violation of CFE provisions. Russia has halted verification visits since June 2007 and insists that it is no longer obliged by treaty to limit its conventional weapons.

In a partially emollient response, NATO initially endorsed a "parallel actions package" in March 2008, calling for Alliance countries nevertheless to begin the ACFE ratification process, while Russia was expected and exhorted to have commenced its required withdrawals. It was hoped that Russia would resolve its issues with Georgia and Moldova, and NATO nations could then quickly complete ratification of the ACFE Treaty and address additional Russian security concerns.

Russia rejected that expectation, and chances of agreement have since been further undermined by the August 2008 conflict with Georgia, Moscow's decision in the same month to recognize South Ossetia and Abkhazia as independent nations, and its continuing refusal to accept any reference to "host nation consent" as a fundamental principle.

In the course of 2010 attempts made towards resuscitation, several bilateral as well as multilateral meetings (using the formula 30+6, 30 CFE members and 6 non-CFE NATO members) took place. Russia and NATO submitted new proposals on escaping the deadlock, "although statements from both sides indicated little chance of agreement."[9] Yet, as a result of post-Cold War military reductions, actual holdings of TLE are in almost all cases well below permitted ceilings.

All this has created a continuing long-term log jam between NATO and Russia, leaving CFE on life support with a diplomatic crisis approaching in the form of a Review Conference required before the end of the year.

THE BALANCE OF INTERESTS

What are the apparent balances of interest in reanimating, adapting, and preserving the gains of CFE inside such a framework?

Benefits to NATO.

There are multiple reasons for NATO to want to preserve CFE.

- Arms Control is a continuing Alliance imperative. At least among European allies, public opinion, above all in Germany, would be alarmed and unforgiving if NATO appeared to be giving up on any hope of reviving ACFE.
- Ostentatious concern to preserve (or perfume) the corpse of CFE may be essential to prevent dissension over NATO's *nuclear* deterrence posture, which is now being examined in the

Alliance's Deterrence and Defence Posture Review (DDPR).

- It would seem, at least to those Westerners who are aware of the issue, axiomatically important to preserve the system of military transparency as widely as possible in Europe. Collapse of the CFE Treaty would damage European arms control in general, all institutions and instruments and the transnational networks of experts, and trained specialist military observers dealing with cooperative security.
- It is uncertain whether the Vienna Document 1999 procedures on confidence and security-building measures[10] could survive if the CFE Treaty were formally declared dead by all parties.
- But similar pessimism over the Dayton Accords would not seem to be justified. They are buttressed by local and Balkan-wide regional pressures and incentives from NATO and the European Union (EU) which are probably sufficiently powerful to hold the present situation together even in the absence of CFE.

Russia and ACFE: General Difficulty and Specific Objections.

Russia's overall problem is that CFE originally codified rough parity at a moment of rough balance between the Warsaw Pact and the West, amid honeymoon expectations of closer and closer security relations. Adapted CFE would have to be agreed, evolved, and applied indefinitely in a situation of undisguiseable and probably growing disparity between a Russia without close military allies and an expanded 28-nation NATO, and where security partnership between NATO and Russia is frequently proclaimed as an objective but is far from apparent.

Specific Russian objections are loud and numerous. The Russian Government now appears to be demanding:[11]

- ratification of the 1999 ACFE Treaty by the NATO states;
- rapid accession of Estonia, Latvia, and Lithuania to the ACFE and their early ratification, to restrict emergency deployments of NATO forces there;
- definition of the term "substantial combat forces" which would limit the forces which the Alliance could introduce into the new NATO states;
- immediate renegotiation and modernization of ACFE if it were ever, temporarily, brought into force;
- balance of some kind between Russian and NATO forces through a "compensatory lowering" of overall NATO ceilings on Treaty limited equipment to take account of NATO's 1999 and 2004 enlargements and the presence of American forces in new NATO nations;
- rejection of the principle of Host Nation Consent to limit Russian deployments. Russia considers the vexed troop withdrawal issues bilateral Russian-Georgian or Russian-Moldovan questions, not relevant to European arms control; and,
- the abolition of "discriminatory" flank restrictions on Russian territory (which especially affect the volatile North Caucasus) by means of a "political decision" between NATO and Russia as necessary strategic compensation for NATO enlargement.

Given the vigor with which Putin denounced CFE in 2007, there is now a self-inflicted restriction on Russian freedom of political maneuver, because concessions in this area could easily be perceived as loss of machismo in election years.

Benefits to Russia.

But without CFE, Russia would lose transparency over the forces of existing or future members of a much larger and militarily superior Alliance and, above all, any legal limits on the deployment of NATO forces into the territory of the three geopolitically crucial Baltic Republics which are not parties to CFE and yet are so neurologically close to St. Petersburg and Russia's "Window on Europe."

SOLUTIONS

A range of compromises designed to save the CFE process have been ingeniously charted by Professor Jeffrey McCausland and others.[12]

Summary of Options.

Option 1. *Continue the current policy of seeking parallel actions by NATO members and Russia leading to a resumption of Russian CFE implementation and a move toward the ACFE Treaty, with some additional inducements to Moscow,* perhaps by: a) declaring overall lower territorial and national ceilings, with only political effect until the ACFE entered into force; or by, b) including the geopolitically crucial Baltic States, in particular, declaring their future territorial and national ceilings.

Option 2. *Continue current policies while opening the ACFE Treaty to amendment*. As a variant, NATO could begin to address Russian concerns over flank limitations, providing Russia showed signs of restarting its implementation of CFE and began serious treaty-related negotiations with Georgia and Moldova. NATO allies could decide to offer discussion of flank limits in the framework of the parallel actions package.

Option 3. *Begin provisional application of the ACFE Treaty, but with conditions*. The Alliance could provisionally apply ACFE among its 10 members for, say, 18 months, in the hope of reciprocation from Russia through resumption of her implementation, and progressive satisfaction of the Istanbul Commitments.

Option 4. *Cease implementing the CFE Treaty and manage a "soft landing" for the end of the CFE regime*. NATO allies could signal to Russia that they had lost confidence in the parallel actions package or in any other potential negotiated solution. Consequently, if Russia continued its refusal to resume implementation of the existing treaty or to negotiate over forces in Georgia and Moldova, NATO would allow the Treaty to die—perhaps without formal ending. To soften the impact on the international landscape, this position could, however, be combined with attempts to persuade all CFE states' parties to make political commitments to continue observing CFE treaty ceilings.

Near Term Prospects.

What might now realistically happen? Previous European arms control experience, and statements by both sides, suggest that it would be unrealistic to expect ACFE to be re-examined, ratified, or otherwise revived *unless* it can be incorporated into a wider U.S.

Russian rapprochement—nearly certain to be dominated by nuclear aspects, as before.

Discussion in NATO related conferences between March and May 2011 suggested that, while this would certainly be a demanding condition, it may not be entirely impossible. In particular, a well-informed yet still optimistic diplomat in the mission of a major ally repeatedly argued that the crucial inducement would be Russia's hope of getting access to advanced U.S. MD technologies through some kind of sharing arrangement. Others suggest that the additional nuclear security advantages of getting some control over the potential upload of U.S. strategic systems in a further treaty would add to the incentive for Russia at least to go through the motions of reopening the process to adapt CFE.

CFE's prospects consequently depend on the Russian leadership seeing a positive outcome from entering overlapping negotiations over nuclear reductions (in both Central Strategic and Theatre Nuclear Weapons, including upload capacity and weapons in storage), MDs, and Conventional Forces in Western Eurasia. This would amount to a tentative military-technical confirmation of long sought Russo—American reset.

It is presumably in recognition of these interactions that responsibility for CFE is widely rumored to be transferred to Rose Gottemoeller's already impressively full State Department negotiating portfolio as Assistant Secretary in the Bureau of Arms Control, Verification and Compliance. Sergey Kislyak, Russia's Ambassador to the United States, stated to Mrs. Gottemoeller at the Carnegie Nuclear Conference in March 2011 that Russia was open to such a multiple negotiation process addressing strategic and theater nuclear weapons, missile defenses, and conventional forces.

If the political hurdles to setting up the negotiations could be surmounted, as these overtures tantalisingly suggest, the actual negotiating complexities would, of course, remain formidable: huge and novel verification difficulties, and difficulties in gaining agreeement for the counting methodologies that will define the balance between diverse conventional forces, or, harder still, between conventional and nuclear forces. (MBFR, as a whole, illustrated how long a stalemate could be maintained over relatively simple issues such as numbers of militarily identical counting units, e.g., numbers of troops or main battle tanks; while attempts by NATO to trade-off Soviet tank units for the withdrawal of American tactical nuclear weapons came to nothing.) Russia's aspiration would be towards a wide scale multiple rebalancing with NATO. There is little public, or academic, indication of new efforts to think through the fundamental methodological problems involved.

Still, while scientifically exact calculations may be impossible, a "good enough equivalency" in a wide scale multiple rebalancing might be agreed upon as the de facto objective. Even the preliminaries to an ambitious forward-looking negotiation of that kind could have attractions in confidence building and creation of a positive diplomatic atmosphere.

Longer-term Possibilities.

At best, revival of CFE to allow ratification of ACFE would mean formal, legalistic, and short-lived transitional steps to a very slow substantive new negotiation. Even going that far would, however, undoubtedly encounter intra-alliance difficulties, though the anxieties of flank allies might be diminished by more assured reinforcements and continuous improvement in electronics, unmanned airpower, precision weapons, and reinforcement planning. But these developments would also have to be addressed in the negotiations. An ACFE follow-on agreement would probably look very different: as much of a transformation as CFE was to MBFR.

If a new negotiation could be started, it might be possible to reach compromises on numbers and even flank limits. But it will be harder to relent on the principal of host country consent, which is integral to both the current and ACFE treaties. The ACFE Treaty would never have been signed if Russia had not first signed the bilateral agreements involving withdrawal from Georgia and Moldova.[13]

There is no public indication of compromises which may have been formulated by the United States to coax Russia back into a conventional arms control process. But diplomatic ingenuity and high-minded fudging might offer sufficient promise within an inevitably long and complex negotiation, cross linked with parallel high stakes U.S.-Russian nuclear and missile defense talks.

CORRELATIONS OF FORCES AND ARMS CONTROL METHODOLOGY

Certain issues raised by conventional arms control in Europe have wider implications. Part of the unpredictability of the CFE decision, and indeed wider uncertainties about Russia's future strategic choices, derives from uncertainties in understanding how others see the effects of military power outside of warfare. This differs from the abstract military-on-military calculations of the impact of arms control proposals on combat outcomes, which are complex enough.

It appears publicly difficult to acknowledge, and even more to agree upon, the significance of what Russian commentators continue to call, even after the end of sophisticated Marxist theories of conflict, the balance or "correlation" of forces: political and psychological force fields generated *in peacetime or incipient crisis* by military power, which may differ from the predicted utility of forces in professional military calculations. To give one recent example:

> The Russian government considered various alternatives of rendering aid in [the 2008 Georgian] situation. After study of the correlation (or balance) of forces and the tactical situation several years in advance of August 2008, the necessity became evident for direct military intervention if the Georgian army undertook an attack on Tskhinvali.[14]

The literature of arms control does not easily capture this aspect. Formally, ACFE or its successor would solely affect the top level of Professor Joseph Nye's now famous three-dimensional 21st-century security chess board, which involves in addition to military power, successively, economic power on the next level down and nongovernmental organizational (NGO) activities and cultural flows below that.[15] ACFE would limit and oversee a set-up of military counters on that top playing surface which would be deliberately and explicitly intended to make successful ground offensives harder to conduct and therefore less potentially psychologically significant. In general, Western politicians and analysts tend to doubt the utility of power constellations on the top board in radiating influence down to the other nonmilitary political, economic, and playing surfaces, and it is not generally discussed in public statements. Even so, there is some informal acknowledgement of this factor, in the discourse of reassurance of exposed allies. A senior NATO official repeatedly emphasised that "we use nuclear weapons every day" in influencing Eurasian geopolitics to wage deterrence and assurance. Presumably, conventional force balances have analogous psychological effects.

Russian perceptions are neither likely to mirror image NATO's, nor to put a lower political value on military numbers. Conventional arms control in Europe now seems to depend, in the near term at least, on Russian conclusions about the impact of ACFE and associated negotiations on the Correlation of Forces affecting Russia's preservation as a Great Power. Decisions on entering some large-scale holistic negotiation will form part of Russia's latest iteration of its fateful national choice of either trust in or suspicion of the West.

It cannot be easy to determine the best way of inhibiting what Russia frequently denounces as relentless pressures from NATO—800 million rich, well-armed democracy-infatuated and moralistically meddlesome citizens of a super power and its allies—recently attacking the Libyan Regime. The Russians appear genuinely perturbed about the ultimate intentions behind the endless inventiveness of American military power. In the worst case, they indicate their fear that NATO might impose, or try continuously to threaten, "Kosovo style solutions" to future crises by "sixth generation" high-technology, conventional stand-off firepower, capable of decapitation attacks, backed by nuclear missiles and, in the future, MD.[16]

Little in Russia's strategic culture and political history indicates that the present Russian leadership see their Great Power status and regime security being tidily accommodated, insulated from wider political and economic considerations, within hygienic, legally enforceable, Kantian "Euro Atlantic Security Structures," the Holy Grail of the European vision.

Instead, and in relation to their own objectives not necessarily stupidly, Russian decisionmakers are likely to see Eurasian security as a complex, continuously changing mixture of pressures; counterpressures; reciprocal inhibitions; anxieties; intimidation; accommodations; cross-border political and cultural subversion; fomented secessions; orchestrated ethnic minority discontents; externally sponsored color revolutions; self-interestedly subsidized scholarships; cyber offensive and defensive capabilities; technological threats; trade deals; energy dependencies and vulnerabilities; historical emotions, fears, and resentments; intra-Alliance fault lines; and mixes of inducements ranging between negotiated strategic bargains, saber rattling maneuvers, co-optation of decisionmakers, soft loans, and straightforward bribery. This hybrid conception of security, involving endless state competition on many levels with few clear boundaries between peace and war, is one in which the present regime feels itself profoundly threatened (as perhaps alternative politico economic systems in Moscow might not) and required to respond with appropriate vigor. The corollary is that Russia can be described as a "challenging neighbor" by a small outspoken adjacent state.[17]

"From Russia's perspective, the region encompassing the former Soviet republics is its 'sphere of privileged interests,' and Moscow views U.S. and Western expansion in this area as a threat."[18] A positive Correlation of Forces, as existed in relation to Georgia in 2008, is very likely to seem positive in maintaining that sphere[19] and countering that and other threats. But it is not easily reconcilable with the intentions of CFE.

Will Russia's difficult and probably weakening (and most certainly demographically declining) strategic hand seem best strengthened by agreeing to examine progressive merger into postmodern transparency and military predictability within an ACFE follow-on system? Or would Russia maintain the best possible correlation of forces, which could most confidently ensure that its Near Abroad does, in fact, prove to be a privileged sphere of influence, by remaining unconstrained by treaty limits and transparencies, in order to remain (and be perceived as) more capable of launching military actions to support its national interests in that geopolitical zone, as it did in 2008 against Georgia?

Russia's leaders may therefore need significant inducements to conclude that, in the foreseeable strategic climate, the impact on the correlation of forces of the potential combined negotiations now on offer would be positive, (and there are likely to be different views on that between Putin and Medvedev and their factions.) Otherwise, a paralysed CFE will continue on life support-which will only be turned off in some way if NATO could risk the painful internal dispute.

Russia's decision over these negotiation packages and possibilities, including an ACFE follow on, will be far reaching and, publicly at least, is still in the balance. But it will not be irreversible. It should be seen as just the latest movement in the long Eurasian strategic dance stretching out into the decades to come.

WIDER ISSUES AND GLOBAL POSSIBILITIES

Current commentary and recent conferences have revealed few reasons to expect a positive change in CFE's prospects in the near future. Nevertheless, whatever choices may emerge from Russia's strategic culture and sense of special predicament and destiny, it is worth looking forward and outward. To call the CFE process mankind's last best hope would clearly be exaggerated, but equally certainly it *has* been the world's most successful attempt so far at reducing military insecurity and suspicion on a continental scale. Secure and peaceful conditions may not have arrived throughout Eurasia (although most parts of Europe are now a security community in which resumption of historical conflicts seem inconceivable), but we should not ignore the moral, political, and human development case for assisting similar movement elsewhere where conditions could become receptive to the benign diplomatic and political technology which was developed during the CFE process.

It has meant that in Europe, with enormous assistance from the United States and frequently positive reactions from Russia, laborious negotiations in Helsinki, Stockholm, Vienna, and elsewhere have created since the 1970s an interlocking system of: force declarations, data exchanges, inspections, discussions of military doctrines, notifications of maneuvers, overflights permitted by an Open Skies Treaty, transnational military specialist communities of inspectors and observers; and, crucially, a Joint Consultative Group to take up and resolve anomalies, directly, promptly, and discreetly. This effort culminated, as we have seen, in the large-scale reductions of forces achieved by CFE, increasing stability and saving tens of millions of dollars.

Confidence and Security Building Measures (CSBM) arrangements in Europe are not perfect or universal and quite evidently not eternal, nor will they necessarily prove to be the only model. But they unquestionably helped transform Europe from the Dark Continent of the early and mid-20th century to the enormously more open, prosperous, and largely demilitarized space that it is today.

This record prompts the question of how the widely internationally applauded goal of Global Zero could ever be achieved without the spread of such arrangements throughout a post-modern world. Most immediately, how realistic is it for diplomats to busy themselves debating the modalities of a Middle East Zone Free of Weapons of Mass Destruction and Their Means of Delivery (MEZFWMD), with the huge problems in trust and verification that implies, if the regional states cannot even agree on how to monitor the declared location and size of an armored division?

It is, however, encouraging that the underreported Conference on Interaction and Confidence Building Measures in Asia (CICA), which is modeled on the OSCE,[20] seems to be willing to examine many of the most positive CSBM lessons from Europe. It may be possible to take the model still further afield. Systematic consideration of how conventional arms control lessons from Europe might be globalized and adapted on other continents in order to make maximum use of inexpensive new aerial surveillance technologies and to contribute to regional security and nation-building, is the subject of a continuing project at the Centre for International Studies and Diplomacy at the School of Oriental and African Studies in London University. Even if baffled and frustrated in its continent of birth, the CFE vision may flourish again in unexpected and exotic regions. But if, in fact, it never does, global expectations for improved international security, economic growth and prosperity will remain seriously bounded.

ENDNOTES - CHAPTER 1

1. See, among other historical analyses, Russell J. Leng, *Interstate Crisis Behaviour, 1816-1980: Realism Vs Reciprocity,"* Cambridge, UK: Cambridge University Press, 1993.

2. Robert Cooper, "The Post Modern State and the World Order" available from *www.demos.co.uk/files/postmodernstate.pdf.*

3. Cooper was not the only writer to see far-reaching significance in CFE: for example, Christopher Coker, "Post-modernity and the end of the Cold War," *Review of International Studies,* July 1992.

4. "Chronology: CFE Treaty Negotiations and Implementation, 1972-1996," Federation of American Scientists, n.d.

5. For the authoritative account of the genesis and nemesis of CFE, see Jane M. O. Sharp, *Striving for Military Stability in Europe: Negotiation, implementation and adaptation of the CFE Treaty,* London, UK: Routledge, 2006.

6. A convenient brief overview is available from *www.armscontrol.org/factsheet/cfe.*

7. Letter of Transmittal to Congress by President William J. Clinton, April 7, 1997.

8. NATO, Questions and Answers on CFE, n.d., p. 2, available from *www.nato.int/nato_static/assets/pdf/pdf_2007_05/20090515_cfe_qa_factsheet.pdf.*

9. Jacek Durkalec, *The Russian Approach towards Revival of Conventional Arms Control Regime in Europe,* Warsaw, Poland: Polish Institute of International Affairs (PISM), November 2010.

10. These are overseen by the OSCE and usefully described in *summit2010.osce.org/en/in_focus/node/248*.

11. V. Socor, *Kremlin Would Re-write Or Kill CFE Treaty*, Washington, DC: The Jamestown Foundation, July 18, 2007.

12. Anne Witkowsky, Sherman Garnett, and Jeff McCausland, *Salvaging the Conventional Armed Forces in Europe Treaty Regime: Options for Washington*, Washington, DC: The Brookings Institute, March 2010, available from *www.brookings.edu/~/media/Files/rc/papers/2010/03_armed_forces_europe_treaty/03_armed_forces_europe_treaty.pdf*.

13. Peter Perenyi, "Key CFE Obstacles are Not 'Subregional'," *Arms Control Today*, December 2009, available from *armscontrol.org*.

14. Anton Lavrov, Moscow Defense Brief #2, No. 24, 2011, available from *mdb.cast.ru/mdb/2-2011/item3/article1/*.

15. See the explication of this fashionable model available from *www.hks.harvard.edu/news-events/news/commentary/american-power-21st-century*.

16. Russian Army General Staff Deputy Head Major General Igor Sheremet, interviewed on Ekho Moskvy radio and reported in Global Security Newswire, May 31, 2011: "We forecast that by 2020 Western countries will be armed with about 80,000 cruise missiles, including about 2,000 with nuclear warheads. . . . It is clear that such arsenals are being created [not] just for exercises or intimidation. These weapons are quite capable of disarming and decapitation strikes," available from *gsn.nti.org/gsn/nw_20110531_9890.php*. To the extent that this view is genuinely held and not simply projected, especially over the improbably large nuclear statistic, to support Russian diplomatic positions, it must be unclear how CFE (which does not, for example, apply at all to the new and explosively expanding weapons category of unmanned aerial vehicles [UAVs]) or other negotiations would reduce Russian concerns about endless Western military-technical fertility.

17. Interview with Mart Laar, Estonia's Minister of Defence, *Jane's Defence Weekly*, July 6, 2011.

18. Steve Andreasen and Michael Gerson, "Deterrence Seen through the Eyes of Other Nations," In George P. Shultz, Sidney D. Drell, and James E. Goodby, eds., *Deterrence Its Past and Future*, Stanford, CA: Hoover Institution Press, Stanford University, 2011, p. 107.

19. The political and strategic costs and distortions for Russia involved in the concept of "a privileged sphere of interests" are discussed in Dmitri Trenin, *Post Imperium-A Eurasian Story*, Washington, DC: Carnegie Endowment For International Peace, 2011.

20. See the Website of the Secretariat on Conference on Interaction and Confidence Building Measures in Asia (CICA), available from *www.s-cica.org/page.php?page_id=7&lang=1*.

CHAPTER 2

EUROPEAN/EURASIAN SECURITY AND THE TREATY ON CONVENTIONAL ARMED FORCES IN EUROPE

Jeffrey D. McCausland

The Treaty on Conventional Armed Forces in Europe (often referred to as the CFE Treaty) was signed in Paris, France, on November 19, 1990, between members of the North Atlantic Treaty Organization (NATO) and the Warsaw Pact. At its signing, many analysts hailed it as "the cornerstone of European security," and it is clearly the most ambitious and far-ranging conventional arms control treaty in history. It underscored a transformation of European security that is still ongoing and whose end state is unclear.[1]

The events that framed this transformation were largely peaceful and remarkable. Only a year before on November 9, 1989, the Berlin Wall, which had served as perhaps the primary symbol of the Cold War for nearly 40 years, was breached. Six weeks prior to the Paris signing, Germany formally reunified into a single nation. The 22 nations that signed this agreement have now subsequently increased to 34. One of the alliances, the Warsaw Pact, has dissolved and the other, NATO, has enlarged. A key signatory to this agreement, the Soviet Union, disappeared and was replaced by a host of successor states. Finally, the nations that convened in Paris did so under the overall auspices of the Conference on Security Cooperation in Europe (CSCE). This organization has now grown to 56 members and become the Organization for Security and Co-operation in Europe (OSCE), which reflects that it has now matured into an international organization. An adapted treaty that reflects many of these political changes was signed on November 19, 1999, at the OSCE Summit held in Istanbul, Turkey, but at this moment it still has not been ratified by the majority of the states involved. All must ratify for it to formally enter into force. At this writing, the treaty is endangered by the lack of progress in ratifying the adapted agreement and a decision by the Russian Federation to suspend compliance.

This obviously begs several important questions that will be examined as part of this analysis. What is the role of the CFE Treaty as part of contemporary European security architecture? How has it performed since its signing and what is its current status? Finally, what steps must be taken to ensure that this agreement remains relevant and continues its "cornerstone" role?

NATIONAL INTEREST, STRATEGY, AND ARMS CONTROL

As we consider how the CFE Treaty fits into emerging European security architecture, it is important to consider first principles. What is the fundamental relationship between national interest, strategy, and arms control? Thucydides noted in his *History of the Peloponnesian War* that a primary motivator of Athenian foreign policy had been "*interests.*"[2] This remains as true for nations in the 21st century as for the city-states of ancient Greece. It is critical to underscore the point that arms control is not an "interest" or objective of state policy. Rather it is a "method or a way" to achieve the objective of improved security which is an essential interest to any state. Though the focus of any negotiation is the details of the prospective agreement, the arms control process must always remain consistent with a nation's interests and the direction of national or alliance security strategy.

Strategic thinking has been the purview of European diplomats at least since the Congress of Vienna. Klemens von Metternich, Charles Maurice Talleyrand, Otto von Bismarck, or Robert Stewart Castlereagh, would all agree that the national strategy of any country is built upon three variables: First, what are the "ends" of strategy or the goals or objectives the nation is trying to accomplish alone or in concert with friends and allies? Second, what are the "ways" or policies that are formulated to move the nation in the direction of a better future? Finally, what are the "means" or resources available to the government of any nation that can be devoted to securing these objectives, and how can they be husbanded in a fashion to maximize their potential?

As a result, modern European policymakers would agree that a connection exists between arms control and each nation's respective national security strategy. Both arms control and military operations are "ways" to achieve national strategic objectives or "ends." But at its very core, any arms control agreement depends upon a harmony of interests among the signatories that is consistent with their respective national interests and associated strategy. This harmony is based on careful analysis by each state that the benefits to be gained from entering the regime outweigh the risks associated with reducing military forces and accepting a transparency regime that includes data exchanges and verification inspections. As a result, an implicit aspect of any multilateral arms control agreement is the "indivisibility" of security. The security of any state, no matter how large or small, is of equal importance. This is clearly reflected in the CFE Treaty by the fact that the initial treaty and any adapted agreement cannot enter into force until all states parties have ratified it. Efforts to overcome the current impasse over the CFE Treaty are in many ways a search for harmony among the signatories.

Consequently, an arms control agreement is neither good nor bad when examined in isolation. Each treaty or agreement only has value as a policy "way" when there are underlying security concerns that, if mitigated, might reduce the possibility of conflict. This is why we do not see arms control agreements being discussed or promulgated between countries that have friendly relations. It is also why we have seen some agreements lapse when security conditions changed.

This also may be why it is often easy to dismiss the success of arms control, since we lose sight of its intent. A successful agreement is one that contributes to the prevention of conflict and enhances stability. But it is hard to correlate completely the cause and effect of policies and apply metrics against something that did not happen. The end of the Cold War, demise of the Soviet Union, collapse of the Warsaw Pact, and emergence of new nations and actors in Europe over the past 20 years all occurred without violence. War did occur in the former Yugoslavia, but this region was outside the area of application of the CFE Treaty, and Yugoslavia did not participate in the treaty process. It is not hard to imagine that such a period of upheaval could have resulted in major conflicts, but this did not occur. Consequently, it is important to remind ourselves that the level of transparency achieved by the CFE Treaty is particularly valuable and astonishing when one considers the security situation in Europe

25 years ago. In many ways this agreement has made the extraordinary routine.

Finally, arms control depends to some degree on other variables. Arms control is a political activity and cannot be divorced from other aspects of a nation's security/foreign policy or domestic agenda. Internal events, other issues between states, and the bureaucratic process of the participating parties have a direct bearing on how an agreement is negotiated and complied with.

THE ORIGINAL CFE TREATY AND ITS ADAPTATION

Conventional arms negotiations between NATO and Warsaw Pact countries first began with the Mutual and Balanced Force Reduction Talks (MBFR) that commenced in Vienna, Austria, in 1973. These discussions accomplished very little and were replaced in 1987 with the CFE negotiations. Despite the failure of MBFR, NATO and the Warsaw Pact negotiators successfully crafted the CFE Treaty in the 3 years between 1987 and 1990.

As a result, many commentators have argued that these negotiations had been successful, while MBFR had failed because a new, more effective formula for the talks had been discovered. This is totally untrue. The real difference between 1973 and 1987 is that in 1973 neither the United States nor the Soviet Union truly wanted an agreement. The Richard Nixon administration entered these discussions largely to defuse efforts in the U.S. Senate to unilaterally reduce American forces based in Europe. The Kremlin entered the negotiations as a tool to try to drive a wedge between Washington and its European allies. By 1987, however, conditions had changed. Soviet leader Mikhail Gorbachev realized that he needed a treaty to reduce the economic burden of deploying large conventional forces in Eastern Europe and as part of his efforts to reform the crumbling Soviet Union.

As stated above, the 22 members of NATO and the Warsaw Pact signed the Treaty on CFE on November 19, 1990, following 3 years of negotiations. It established limits on the aggregate total of conventional military hardware for the two blocs, required substantial reductions in each nation's conventional arsenal, and created an intrusive regime of inspections and verification.

The talks commenced in January 1988 and the following mandate was agreed upon to guide these negotiations:

> The objectives of the negotiation shall be to strengthen stability and security in Europe through the establishment of a stable and secure balance of conventional armed forces, which include conventional armaments and equipment, at lower levels; the elimination of disparities prejudicial to stability and security; and the elimination, as a matter of priority, of the capability for launching surprise attack and for initiating large scale offensive action.[3]

The final agreement required alliance or "group" limitations on tanks, artillery, armored combat vehicles (ACVs), combat aircraft, and attack helicopters—known collectively as Treaty Limited Equipment (TLE)—in an area stretching from the Atlantic Ocean to the Ural Mountains. Each bloc was allowed the following:

Treaty Limited Equipment (TLE)	Group Limit
Tanks	20,000
Artillery	20,000
Armored Combat Vehicles (ACVs)	30,000
Attack Helicopters	2,000
Combat Aircraft	6,800

Subsequent national limits for each treaty signatory were determined during negotiations among the members of the two respective alliances. Following the demise of the Soviet Union, the successor states (within the area of treaty application) determined their respective limits from the total allocated to the Soviet Union in May 1992. The three Balkan states (Lithuania, Latvia, and Estonia) did not participate in the discussions of the national limits for the "successor" states of the Soviet Union. They argued that they had been "occupied territory" and, therefore, their territory was no longer part of the treaty's area of application. Still, following their entry into NATO, all of them have indicated a willingness to accede to the Adapted Conventional Forces in Europe (ACFE) Treaty once it enters into force.

Bloc limitations for NATO and the former Warsaw Pact were further restrained by a series of five geographic nested zones for land-based TLE with respective limits for each zone. This was done to achieve the goals established in the mandate to prevent the destabilizing concentration of conventional military armament. The four zones commence with a central region consisting of Germany, the Benelux, Poland, the Czech Republic, Hungary, and Slovakia. The term "nesting" signifies that, beginning with this initial zone, each successive zone subsumes all the preceding zones, plus adjacent states and military districts. Cumulative limits are assigned on holdings of TLE in each zone. This construct has the effect of permitting free movement of equipment and units away from, but not towards, the central European region, which thus inhibits surprise attack in the area deemed, during the Cold War at least, to be the most vulnerable.

The Soviet Union (and subsequently the Russian Federation) further accepted the so-called "flank zone." This portion of the agreement places limits on ground-based systems in the Leningrad and North Caucasus Military Districts in the Russian Federation. Norway is part of the northern portion of the flank, and the north Caucasus states, Turkey, Greece, Bulgaria, Romania, and Moldova are in the southern portion. Limitations on helicopters and attack aircraft only apply to the entire area of application due to their ability to reposition rapidly.

New negotiations began after the signing of the treaty focusing on personnel strength of armed forces. This resulted in the Concluding Act of the Negotiations on Personnel Strength of Conventional Armed Forces in Europe (referred to as the CFE-1A agreement). It was signed on July 6, 1992, and established limits on the personnel strength of military forces, with the exception of sea-based naval units, internal security forces, or those assigned to United Nations (UN) duties. CFE-1A (unlike the CFE Treaty) is a politically binding arrangement as opposed to a legally binding treaty. It provided that the ceilings announced by each signatory would take effect 40 months after entry into force and further contained provisions for information exchange, notification, and verification.

Only 1 year after the signing of the initial agreement and as treaty implementation was commencing, Russian leaders began arguing for adjustments to their equipment limits. They began pressing concerns about Russia's equipment limitations, particularly in the flank region, and Moscow undertook a campaign to alter those limits. A final compromise was achieved at the first Review Conference (May 1996) that permitted Russia higher force levels in the flank zone, established a May 1999 deadline for Moscow to meet these adjusted levels, and reduced the overall size of the flank zone. Still, the problem of Russian force levels in this area would continue to bedevil negotiators. It was exacerbated by Russian military operations in Chechnya (which is in the flank region) and the conflict between Russia and Georgia in 2008. At the same time, treaty signatories had already begun (as agreed at the 1996 CFE Review Conference) to embark on a "modernization" of the treaty to adapt it more broadly to the changed European security architecture, one without a Soviet Union or a Warsaw Pact.

These CFE Treaty adaptation negotiations continued from 1996-99, through a period in which the European landscape continued to evolve. Of direct relevance to the treaty and conventional forces, NATO began its process of enlargement. The enlargement process, together with the dissolution of the Soviet Union, brought to the surface a number of Russian concerns about changes that needed to be made to the treaty. Many are identical in theme to those that Russia is currently raising.

On November 19, 1999 (the ninth anniversary of the CFE Treaty), 30 leaders signed the ACFE Treaty. All 19 NATO members accepted lower cumulative national limits from 89,026 TLE to 79,967. All signatories accepted the new structure of limitations based on national and territorial ceilings, consistent with the principle of host nation consent for the presence of foreign forces on any country's territory. The agreement also provided enhanced transparency through increased quotas for mandatory on-site inspections, operational flexibilities to exceed ceilings temporarily, and an accession clause.

The states parties also adopted the CFE Final Act. This document contains a number of political commitments related to the ACFE Treaty. These commitments are: (1) reaffirmation of Russia's commitment to fulfill existing obligations under the treaty to include equipment levels in the flank region; (2) a Russian commitment to exercise restraint in deployments in its territory adjacent to the Baltic; (3) the commitment by a number of Central European countries not to increase (and in some cases to reduce) their CFE territorial ceilings; and, (4) Moscow's agreement with Georgia and Moldova on the withdrawal of Russian forces from their territories. President Bill Clinton noted in his statement at the conclusion of the summit that he would not submit the agreement for review by the Senate until Russia had reduced to the flank levels set forth in the ACFE Treaty, to include removing its forces from Georgia and Moldova.

The most important agreed change in the ACFE Treaty was that the parties took the old Treaty out of the Cold War framework—eliminating the bloc construct and reflecting the new reality of a Europe no longer divided. The original treaty's group limits were replaced by national and territorial limits governing the TLE of every state's party. The treaty's flank limits were adjusted for Russia, providing Russia considerably more flexibility for deployment of

Armored Combat Vehicles (ACVs) in the Northern and Southern portions of the flank than it had under the original treaty. Corresponding transparency measures, which apply equally to Russia and all other states parties, were a crucial part of this deal. Having taken the group structure out of the treaty to reflect that Europe was no longer divided, Allies and other states parties committed to lowering their ceilings in the ACFE Treaty. These ceilings became more explicit in the ACFE Treaty text and were codified in Istanbul. Actual conventional force levels are well below those ceilings and, in the case of NATO members, well below the original group limits.

Other provisions were adopted to reflect the new security environment. Russia's concerns about the three Baltic republics achieving NATO membership were addressed by adding an accession clause to the ACFE Treaty. As previously mentioned, these states indicated their readiness to request accession once the ACFE Treaty entered into force. The 1997 NATO-Russia Founding Act contained a key sentence to address Russia's concerns about stationed forces on the territory of new member states:

> NATO reiterates that in the current and foreseeable security environment, the Alliance will carry out its collective defense and other missions by ensuring the necessary interoperability, integration, and capability for reinforcement rather than by additional permanent stationing of substantial combat forces.[4]

Throughout this period of the 1990s, the treaty signatories also dealt with a raft of implementation issues—e.g., the flank, and destruction of Russian equipment—and reached, for the most part, a successful resolution to these concerns.

THE RUSSIAN "SUSPENSION"

On December 12, 2007, the Russian Federation officially announced that it would no longer be bound by the restrictions of the 1990 CFE Treaty, and suspended participation.[5] Moscow took this action due to the fact that the 22 NATO members bound by the 1990 agreement have not ratified the 1999 ACFE Treaty, and during a June 2007 extraordinary conference, Russia provided a further detailed list of "negative effects" of the conduct of NATO states.[6] These included overall NATO force levels, the flank limits, and other unspecified demands for additional transparency. In addition to these concerns, it was clear that Prime Minister Vladimir Putin and Russian leaders in general were angry over a series of issues, including NATO enlargement, the independence of Kosovo, and plans to install American anti-ballistic missiles on Polish territory. Nonetheless, Moscow reassured the other treaty signatories that it did not intend to dramatically increase its force levels in the territory adjacent to their borders. Russian President Dmitry Medvedev underscored Russia's seriousness about its Treaty concerns when he described the existing agreement as both "unfair" and "nonviable."[7] At the same time, Russian leaders have been quick to describe the contributions made by the treaty as valuable, and to further acknowledge the spirit of both trust and cooperation that it has engendered.

In terms of ratification, NATO members have argued since the Istanbul Summit in 1999 that their ratification remained contingent upon Russia complying with obligations it freely accepted when the ACFE Treaty was signed, the most contentious being the full removal of all Russian military forces from the territory of the former Soviet republics of Georgia and Moldova. Russia adamantly refutes this linkage and Russian Prime Minister Putin has publicly argued that "there is no legal link" between the ACFE Treaty and these commitments.[8]

Practically speaking, therefore, the Treaty is beginning to unravel. Russia has not provided input as part of the biannual data exchange since it suspended participation in 2007. Nor has Russia provided required information on changes to the location of ground TLE, and it is no longer accepting (nor participating in) the treaty's routine and challenge inspection regime. The implications of this situation for the future health of the CFE Treaty are serious. Although other parties continue to implement the treaty in full, a situation in which Russia is not implementing core treaty provisions cannot be sustained forever. At some point, this state of affairs will cause other states parties to begin reevaluating their own treaty participation. If that becomes the case, the treaty will truly unravel. This will have unforeseen implications not only for the ability to deal with other issues on the bilateral and European security agenda, but also possibly with respect to the defense postures among the states parties, as well as other arms control agreements. Even President Medvedev, in his speech, seemed to have indicated his preference for avoiding the treaty's "complete and final collapse."[9]

In response, NATO endorsed a "parallel actions package" in March 2008 in an attempt to avoid the treaty's demise. The package represented a serious shift in the NATO position, as it called for NATO countries to begin the ratification process (which in some countries such as the United States might take several months), while Russia commenced its withdrawals. Once the forces had been removed from Georgia and Moldova, NATO countries would strive to complete ratification of the ACFE Treaty quickly. NATO members also pledged to address many Russian security concerns once the ACFE Treaty was in place. For example, all new NATO members that are not treaty signatories (Slovenia, Estonia, Latvia, and Lithuania) have agreed to accede. NATO also announced that following final ratification, it would be willing to discuss Russian concerns about future weapons ceilings and limitations placed on Moscow in the so-called "flank zones" that border Turkey, Norway, and the Baltic Republics.[10] Unfortunately, the negotiations made little to no progress between March and August 2008. This effort was largely undermined by the deteriorating relations between NATO countries and the Russian Federation in the aftermath of the conflict in Georgia in the late summer of 2008. In fact, one expert observed that this conflict violated the principles contained in both OSCE documents as well as the preamble to the CFE Treaty. These documents call for states parties to refrain from "the threat or use of force against the territorial integrity or political independence of any State," as well as the commitment to peaceful cooperation and the prevention of military conflict anywhere on the European continent.[11] This situation has been further complicated by Moscow's subsequent decision to recognize South Ossetia and Abkhazia as independent nations.

Following the meeting of OSCE foreign ministers in June 2009, the so-called "Corfu Process" began to examine European security challenges. By early 2010, an effort was undertaken in the Joint Consultative Group to develop a framework document that would simply contain principles of conventional arms control which all nations could agree upon. It was hoped that this would serve as a basis for new negotiations, and in the interim offer each state the option of either complying with the existing CFE Treaty or the list of specific requirements described in the framework document.

At the NATO Summit in Lisbon, Portugal, in November 2010, the Alliance reaffirmed its continued commitment to the CFE Treaty Regime and all associated elements. The Final Communiqué noted that although agreement had not yet been achieved on how to "strengthen and modernize the arms control regime for the 21st Century," progress among the 36 participating states was encouraging. The allies further underscored the indivisibility of security for all states parties and urged continued "efforts to conclude a principles-based framework to guide negotiations in 2011." This process should build "on the CFE Treaty of 1990, the Agreement on Adaptation of 1999, and existing political commitments." While the ultimate goal remained to ensure the continued viability of conventional arms control in Europe and strengthening common security, member states further recognized (as noted at the previous Summit) that "the current situation, where NATO CFE Allies implement the Treaty while Russia does not, cannot continue indefinitely."[12]

Still, little progress has been made, largely due to Russian insistence that it cannot accept any language in the framework document that recognizes host nation consent for stationed forces as an essential principle. It would seem that time is rapidly running out. The treaty requires a Review Conference every 5 years which, in accordance with this provision, should have occurred in 2011. It appears now this will happen in the late fall of 2012. If no agreement can be reached on the framework document, the CFE Treaty may truly be in crisis.

WHAT HAVE BEEN THE CONTRIBUTIONS OF THE CFE TREATY?

As suggested at the onset, the CFE Treaty has long been referred to as the "cornerstone of European security." But in light of the dramatic changes in European security architecture that have occurred since 1991, many wonder if that will continue to be the case and, if so, for how much longer? Obviously this question looms large in the aftermath of the Russian suspension and subsequent conflict between Georgia and the Russian Federation. Can this agreement assist in reestablishing a sense of cooperative security, or have both its credibility and utility been undermined permanently?

Many diplomats and military leaders still believe the treaty continues to be of vital importance to European security. Some argue, however, that its vitality depends upon all states parties accepting the following: (1) The 1990 CFE treaty, with its 1996 flank adjustments, must continue to be fully implemented; and (2) The 1999 ACFE Treaty must be brought into force. Only upon these foundations can the CFE states parties take a forward-looking approach to any additional changes that must be made to continue to ensure this Treaty's viability.

In retrospect, the agreement can only be truly evaluated against the backdrop of European security during this crucial period. Oddly, the treaty was signed to prevent, or at least reduce, the likelihood of conflict between NATO and the Warsaw Pact. Shortly after it was signed, the Warsaw Pact and the Soviet Union both disappeared, so the true value of the treaty must be considered in the context of the dramatic transition that ensued. In fact, some have argued that the "cornerstone" metaphor is misplaced. The CFE Treaty has not been a static agreement—as Europe has weathered many changes, the treaty has been successfully adapted to accommodate those changes.

The treaty clearly proved important in assuaging concerns about German reunification and provided transparency during the withdrawal of massive Soviet forces from Eastern Europe. These withdrawals occurred following the signing of the Treaty on German Reunification (September 12, 1990) by the Federal Republic, the German Democratic Republic (East Germany), France, the United Kingdom (UK), the Soviet Union, and the United States.[13] This agreement also contained significant additional restraints on military operations. Germany agreed to only deploy territorial units that were not integrated in the NATO command structure on the territory of the former East Germany. Bonn further agreed that no foreign troops would be stationed in its eastern states or "carry out any other military activity there" while the withdrawal of Soviet forces was ongoing. Finally, the reunification treaty also specified that "foreign armed forces and nuclear weapons or their carriers will not be stationed in that part of Germany or deployed there," though Germany did insist on the ability to interpret "deployed."[14]

In terms of the actual reductions of military equipment associated with the implementation of the original treaty, the numbers are truly impressive. Over 69,000 Cold War era battle tanks, combat aircraft, and other pieces of military equipment have been destroyed in the now 30 countries stretching from the Atlantic to the Ural Mountains. In many ways, the treaty changed the face of European security by "establishing new, cooperative political-military relationships."[15] More than 5,500 on-site inspections have been conducted, which has created a new sense of political-military cooperation and openness.

The true value of the treaty and the associated transparency measures were demonstrated during the various conflicts in the Balkans. Short notice inspections in accordance with CFE were conducted of U.S. forces in Germany by Russian inspectors as the American troops prepared to depart for Bosnia in 1995. As a result, these military operations were conducted without a significant increase in tensions. The Dayton Accords that ended the initial conflict in the former Yugoslavia in 1996 also contain an annex that established a CFE-like agreement between the contending states. The treaty was crafted to be nearly identical to the CFE Treaty in terms of limits, definitions, transparency measures, etc. All of the Balkan states participating in this agreement expressed a desire to accede to the full CFE Treaty at some point in the future. Finally, in 1999 a Russian inspection was also conducted at Aviano Airbase during the U.S.-led air campaign against Serbian forces in Kosovo. This helped allay to some degree Russian concerns about U.S. force deployments during this crisis.

In fact, many experts believe the inspection regime may have contributed more to the reduction of tensions and crisis prevention during this dramatic transition in European security than the actual reductions. Some argue that the agreement's greatest value may be the entire CFE system that encourages confidence through transparency. In the final analysis, the existing treaty (as well as the adapted agreement) provides a forum for the major European states to debate, agree, and maintain a set of rules about conventional military power on the continent that is critical to overall stability.[16]

WHAT WOULD FAILURE MEAN?

One Russian commentator remarked that the treaty is "a true relic of the Cold War and an example of how outdated agreements negotiated 'a long time ago in a galaxy far, far away' *perpetuate* adversarial relationships."[17] But this opinion is not shared by most treaty members and security experts. A group of distinguished Western diplomats, military leaders, and academics prepared a letter in 2008 that argued that the collapse of the CFE Treaty would ". . . undermine co-operative security in Europe and lead to new dividing lines and confrontations."[18]

So, what would the impact on the future be if the CFE Treaty failed and the flow of routinely provided information on conventional equipment, inspections to verify that information, and constraints on the levels of that equipment were to disappear? What would be both Russian and Western perspectives on a situation in which there were no limits at all on the level and location of conventional weapons deployments or the conventional force levels of treaty signatories? What would the European security picture look like if the habits of cooperation developed through the CFE Treaty were undone?

Sadly, it is not too far-fetched to imagine that this could cause a dramatic realignment of European security. The loss of information and undermining of predictability would set the stage for historic animosities to resurface and lingering crises to potentially worsen. For example, there have been suggestions that Azerbaijan is counting on the failure of the treaty to provide it with an opportunity to increase its military forces. Such a development would clearly exacerbate tensions between Azerbaijan and Armenia. These two countries remain embroiled in a long simmering conflict over Nagorno-Karabakh.[19] This struggle has resulted in over 15,000 casualties since 1988 and over 800,000 Armenian and Azeri refugees. Furthermore, Russia would also lose any transparency over the military forces of existing or future members of the NATO alliance, as well as the deployment of NATO forces on the territory of new members. Finally, the Baltic republics would not be expected to accede to the existing agreement and, consequently, there would be no mechanism to affect transparency about military forces on their territory.

Many believe these developments might encourage an expansion in military forces or damage to other agreements. For example, some experts believe Russia might reconsider its participation in the Intermediate-Range Nuclear Forces (INF) Treaty in an effort to improve its security posture. Russian President Putin threatened such action in a statement in February 2007. Loss of CFE would also remove a valuable crisis management tool from the security architecture and damage arms control as an instrument to enhance overall European stability. In this regard, Balkan observers believe the demise of the CFE Treaty might mean an end to the arms control arrangements contained in the Dayton Accords. Obviously, such a development could contribute to renewed violence in that troubled region.

The collapse of the CFE Treaty could spill over into other aspects of the Russia-NATO relationship as well. CFE's collapse could undermine the cooperative European security structures that have been built over the last 15-plus years. These efforts include the NATO-Russia Council, the OSCE, and prospects for building or enhancing future cooperation in other areas.

Futhermore, if CFE is abandoned, its benefits would be difficult, if not impossible, to replace. It is hard to imagine how to build new arrangements if there is no foundation any more on which to construct them. Beyond that, if CFE is no longer a viable agreement, and the confidence-building aspects of the regime are destroyed completely, over time it is entirely possible that some states parties will seek alternative arrangements that will replace the security benefits they now derive from the treaty.

Finally, the dissolution of this agreement could also have a major impact on relations between the United States and the Russian Federation. Moscow and Washington have had serious disagreements over the past decade and, at the onset of the Barack Obama administration, their bilateral relations were perhaps worse than at any time since the end of the Cold War.[20] Early in the new administration, President Obama called for hitting the "reset button" in the relations between the two countries and, despite serious differences, the two sides were able to negotiate the New Strategic Arms Reduction Treaty (New START) agreement by the spring of 2010. This was subsequently ratified by both the U.S. Senate and the Russian Duma. While there was no explicit link between these negotiations and the CFE Treaty deadlock, it is clear that this success could improve the prospects for finding a resolution to the problem.

WHERE DO WE GO FROM HERE?

As we look to the future, Russian and NATO strategists must carefully consider the deadlock over the CFE Treaty and how conventional arms control more broadly can help reestablish a sense of cooperative security in the aftermath of the Russian-Georgian conflict. Michael Wyganowski, a former Polish diplomat who headed Poland's delegation to the CFE Treaty negotiations in 1999, underscored the importance of the CFE Treaty following the conflict. He observed that the accord was being relegated further to the sidelines by a conflict that actually underscored the importance of limiting conventional arms holdings.[21]

With respect to the future of the CFE Treaty, there are, in principle, three paths ahead. The first option would be the status quo: Russia continues its suspension, and efforts to resolve these issues remain deadlocked. In this scenario, the treaty over time will collapse. Other states parties are unlikely to continue to implement a treaty while Russia continues to avoid its treaty obligations.

The second path is that NATO agrees to address Russian CFE demands and ratifies the ACFE Treaty despite the continued presence of Russian forces in Abkhazia, South Ossetia, and Moldova. This is also unlikely to happen. In July 2007 (1 year prior to the Russian-Georgian War), the U.S. Senate passed Resolution 278. This resolution reaffirmed the Senate's support for the Treaty, described the Russian suspension as "regrettable," and further warned that this was a "step that will unnecessarily heighten tensions in Europe."[22] In this environment, it is very unlikely that the Obama administration would seek Senate ratification of the ACFE Treaty, absent Russian compliance with the Istanbul commitments.

The third path is to continue to seek agreement on the framework document of principles which could set the stage for new negotiations. If this cannot be achieved by the Review Conference in the fall of 2012, it may be an appropriate time for all NATO members to consider adopting the same position that the Russian Federation has taken and suspend the existing CFE Treaty. This should not be seen as an effort to end the treaty or to argue that the Russian Federation is in "material breach." Rather, it would simply be an acknowledgement that, after 4 years, the Alliance cannot continue to fulfill treaty obligations absent some reciprocity from Moscow. NATO members could simply state that the framework discussions are a good start and should continue. Still after 4 years of effort, it would appear these negotiations are at an impasse. A decision to at least temporarily halt the discussion of implementation of the ACFE Treaty or compliance with the existing treaty might clear the agenda and allow other areas of mutual interest between Russia and NATO to be discussed.

Clearly, a number of the core Russian concerns can best be addressed not by the wholesale abandonment of CFE, but the opposite, through entry into force of the ACFE Treaty or new negotiations. The ACFE Treaty provides the means through which Russia can ensure predictability in the levels and locations of NATO forces, as well as a means of inspecting these forces against the information that NATO provides. Consequently, a decision by Moscow to move in the direction of compromise would not be based on altruism but rather on a careful calculation of Russian national interest. Russian Foreign Minister Sergey Lavrov seemed to reflect this in remarks at the Council on Foreign Relations in New York when he observed, "the only thing we want internationally is cooperation on the basis of full equality and mutual benefit."[23] Still, it is unclear whether all of the Russian concerns can be resolved within the context of the CFE Treaty. Moscow has also recommended a new Pan-European

Security agreement. Consequently, it would seem more likely that resolution to the disagreement over the CFE Treaty might be a valuable precursor that would allow for serious negotiations on a number of European security issues to occur.

CONCLUSIONS

A Western arms control expert once remarked that he felt like he was watching 300 years of European hostilities unfold during the course of CFE negotiations. Critics of this process are frequently captivated by the technical details of definitions, counting rules, stabilizing measures, inspection regimes, etc., and often overlook the connection between these points and larger security issues. Still while the "devil may lie in the details," this accord is rooted in the collective attempt of over 30 sovereign states to improve their respective security. Consequently, historical antagonisms have an impact, as well as contributing to the agreement's enduring value as Europe seeks a new architecture based on cooperative security.

With the rising threat of transnational issues such as nuclear proliferation and terrorism, the fate of conventional weapons in Europe may not top the priority agenda of the NATO or Russian leadership. But while the original purpose of the treaty—to reduce the risk of conflict and short-warning attacks between two blocs—may be a thing of the past, the CFE Treaty continues to contribute to Europe's security in crucial ways. Perhaps most importantly, the transparency and predictability that it provides serve as important stabilizing elements as European relationships continue to evolve and military forces are modernized.

As we consider the way ahead, it may be useful to examine the thoughts of Hans Morgenthau, one of the most celebrated scholars of international relations in the 20th century. Morgenthau observed the following three points when considering diplomacy and state policy: First, diplomacy must be rescued from crusading spirits. Second, diplomacy must look at the political scene from the point of view of other nations. Third, the objective of foreign policy must be defined in terms of national interests and supported by adequate power.[24]

Russia and the West must avoid emotional rhetoric. Both sides must rely on the kind of careful analysis Morgenthau suggests in order to discover if a harmony of interests still exists. They must carefully consider the major areas of cooperation where long-term interests clearly overlap on issues such as international terrorism, energy, nonproliferation of weapons of mass destruction, and stability in Europe.[25] Alliance members should closely review the Alliance Strategic Concept that was signed in 1999. This document observed that arms control continues to have ". . . a major role in the achievement of the Alliance's security and objectives in the future."[26] Russian negotiators should carefully consider the comments by Russian President Medvedev. He observed that though relations between Russia and the West had experienced critical situations, still "in the end, common sense, pragmatism, and mutual interests will always prevail."[27]

ENDNOTES - CHAPTER 2

1. Dorn Crawford, *Conventional Armed Forces in Europe, (CFE) – A Review and Update of Key Treaty Elements*, Washington: U.S. Department of State, March 2009, p. 2.

2. Charles Robinson, *Greek and Roman Historians*, New York: Holt, Rinehart, and Winston, Inc., 1957, p. 71.

3. Crawford, p. 5.

4. Zdzislaw Lachowski, "The CFE Treaty One Year After Its Suspension: A Forlorn Treaty?" SIPRI Policy Brief, January 2009, p. 1.

5. *Ibid.*, p. 4.

6. Wade Boese, "Russia Unflinching on CFE Treaty Suspension," *Arms Control Today*, May 2008.

7. *Ibid.*

8. Lachowski, p. 5.

9. NATO Public Diplomacy Division, "Press Release—Lisbon Summit Declaration," Brussels, Belgium: NATO Public Affairs, November 20, 2010, p. 9.

10. "Treaty on the Final Settlement with Respect to Germany," *NATO Review*, No. 5, October 1990, pp. 30-32.

11. "Fact Sheet—Treaty on Conventional Armed Forces in Europe (CFE): Key Facts About the Current Treaty and Agreement on Adaptation," Washington, DC: Department of State, 2009.

12. Sherman Garnett, "The CFE Flank Agreement," Washington, DC: The Carnegie Endowment for International Peace, 1997, p. 1.

13. Lachowski, p. 6. This view was underscored by senior Georgian officials during discussions in Tbilisi, Georgia, in December 2010.

14. Dmitri Trenin, "Thinking Strategically About Russia," Washington, DC: Carnegie Endowment for International Peace, December 2008, p. 1.

15. Wade Boese, "Georgian Conflict Clouds Future Arms Pacts," *Arms Control Today*, September 2008.

16. Hans Morgenthau and Kenneth Thompson, *Politics Among Nations*, 6th Ed., New York: McGraw-Hill, 1985, p. 165.

17. David C. Speedie, "U.S.-Russia Relations: Under Stress, and In Need of Care," Carnegie Council for Ethics in International Affairs, available from *cceia.org/resources/articles_papers_reports/0005.html*.

18. *NATO Strategic Concept*, Washington, DC: North Atlantic Council, April 23, 1999.

19. Thom Shanker, "Gates Urges Cautious NATO Stance on Russia After Georgian Conflict," *New York Times*, September 19, 2008, p. A5.

20. Trenin, p. 1.

21. Boese.

22. U.S. Senate, "Expressing the sense of the Senate regarding the announcement of the Russian Federation of its suspension or implementation of the Conventional Armed Forces in Europe Treaty. (Agreed to by the Senate)," 110th Cong., 2st sess., July 24, 2007, Washington, DC.

23. Russian Foreign Minister Sergey Lavrov, Interview with David Remnick, Council on Foreign Relations, New York, September 24, 2008.

24. Morgenthau and Thompson, p. 165.

25. Speedie.

26. *NATO Strategic Concept*.

27. Shanker, p. A5.

CHAPTER 3

EUROPEAN SECURITY AND ARMS CONTROL

Sergey Rogov

The European security situation could be seriously aggravated as Europe slides toward a new division. The arms control regime, which was negotiated at the end of the Cold War era and has been considered the backbone of international security, faces unprecedented threats.

The Western powers never had a strategy to integrate Russia into the community of democratic market countries after the end of the Cold War. There was a strategy to integrate Eastern Europe, and after that the Baltic states, but Moscow was never invited to join key Western institutions: the North Atlantic Treaty Organization (NATO) and the European Union (EU). This led to a new division of Europe.

The arms control regime is facing serious challenges. The United States unilaterally withdrew from the Anti-Ballistic Missile (ABM) Treaty in 2002. Meanwhile, Russia announced a "moratorium" on the Conventional Armed Forces in Europe (CFE) Treaty. Russia also is displeased with the Intermediate Range Nuclear Forces (INF) Treaty, which banned medium and shorter range nuclear missiles.

Two decades after the end of the Cold War, Russia and the West once again confront each other on a number of issues. The disagreements accumulate and may have dangerous consequences which can be devastating for both sides. Russia will hardly become a democracy and a modern market economy if there is a new confrontation with the Western Allies. The

West may antagonize a valuable partner for European and global stability at the moment when it faces an unprecedented American debacle in Iraq and Afghanistan, and while China and India boldly gain a growing importance in the international system.

But it is premature to write off the strategic partnership between Russia and the West. The New Strategic Arms Reduction Treaty (New START) establishes predictability and stability of the nuclear balance for the next decade within the paradigm of mutual nuclear deterrence. This will help to change the strategic paradigm and eventually move to mutually assured security.

Although some disagreements will persist, both sides can still make new solid arrangements for cooperation in the security area for mutual benefit. These cooperative measures should deal with at least three issues:

1. Modernizing the arms control regime;
2. Coordinating Ballistic Missile Defense (BMD) efforts; and,
3. Jointly resisting the victory of the Taliban in Afghanistan.

EVOLUTION OF THE CONVENTIONAL ARMS CONTROL REGIME IN EUROPE

While most of the arms control treaties have been bilateral agreements between Washington and Moscow, the CFE Treaty is a multilateral regime, which is vitally important for Europeans. Its collapse may lead to an unrestricted arms race in Europe.

During the Cold War, NATO and the Warsaw Pact maintained huge conventional armed forces in Europe, ready to immediately confront each other, so the immediate purpose of the CFE Treaty was to prevent a surprise attack. That was particularly important for the Western Allies, because the Warsaw Pact members enjoyed a substantial superiority in military personnel and most types of conventional arms, with the Soviet Union having more weapons than all NATO countries combined.

The CFE Treaty, negotiated together with the first Strategic Arms Reduction Treaty (START) and INF treaties, was a very elaborate and complicated arrangement which was based on the principle of numerical parity, originally accepted in 1972 when the Union of Soviet Socialist Republics (USSR) and the United States signed the ABM treaty and Strategic Arms Limitations Talks (SALT) agreement, and which was confirmed in the SALT, START, and INF treaties.

The CFE also established a unique transparency regime, which included comprehensive verification and monitoring measures, including exchange of information and onsite inspections. But almost immediately after it was signed in November 1990, the CFE Treaty was overtaken by the drastic political landslide in Europe. The Warsaw Pact was dissolved, Germany was reunited, and the Soviet Union disappeared. Nevertheless, the CFE came into force and its key provisions, including destruction of 62,000 heavy weapons, mostly by former Warsaw Pact members, and the transparency regime, were implemented. The only problem was Russia's inability to reduce its forces in the flank zones, which related to the war in Chechnya.

All former members of the Warsaw Pact, except former Soviet republics, plus Estonia, Latvia, and Lithuania, joined the North Atlantic alliance. The military and political balance in Europe fundamentally changed. NATO became the dominant military and political factor.

According to the NATO-Russia Founding Act in 1997, the North Atlantic alliance made a political commitment to avoid a substantial deployment of foreign conventional forces and nuclear weapons in the territories of the new member-states. The new European reality was partially reflected in the Adapted Conventional Armed Forces in Europe (ACFE) Treaty signed in November 1999 in Istanbul, Turkey, when aggregate block ceilings were abandoned and replaced by national quotas. Regional ceilings, except for the flank zones, were also eliminated, although NATO agreed to raise the levels for the Northern Caucasus and Leningrad, Russia, military districts.

Nevertheless, the ACFE Treaty was not ratified by NATO countries, because Russia failed to implement its commitment made in Istanbul and to remove military bases from Georgia and Moldova.

Russia ratified the ACFE Treaty in 2004. But after Washington decided to deploy BMD in Eastern Europe, Russia insisted on an emergency meeting of all member-states of the CFE Treaty, where it demanded to eliminate the flank zones completely and insisted on some other concessions from NATO. After these demands were rejected, Moscow announced a "moratorium."

Thus the very existence of the CFE Treaty is jeopardized since, without Russia, the conventional arms control regime in Europe makes no sense at all.

WHAT'S WRONG WITH THE CFE TREATY?

There is no doubt that the CFE Treaty completely lost its *raison d'être*. There is no way to maintain the numerical parity between NATO and the nonexistent Warsaw Pact. There is no threat of a surprise attack in

Europe. Today all Russian forces in Europe are much smaller than the Soviet forces in all of East Germany 2 decades ago.

One can raise a number of questions, criticizing the provisions of the original and the ACFE Treaty, which seem unnecessary and even counterproductive.

1. The CFE ceilings are too high. For instance, the original CFE Treaty established the combined limit of 40,000 tanks for all participants. The Adapted CFE level is 36,000. This is two times more than were in Europe during World War II, after the invasion of Normandy. There is no scenario for the employment of all these tanks except a new all-European war involving NATO and Russia. All of the latest military conflicts, where CFE member-states participated, involved no tanks at all (Kosovo), a few dozen (Afghanistan), or a few hundred (Chechnya, Iraq). Thus the CFE justifies maintenance in Europe of huge force structures, relying on tanks and other heavy weapons. European countries spend dozens of billions of Euros each year to preserve these useless weapons, while a very small sum is allocated for rapid deployment forces, which are much more relevant for peacekeeping and Global War on Terror (GWOT) operations like in Afghanistan and Darfur.

The legal ceilings for five types of weapons for NATO have grown as a result of CFE adaptation from 20,000 to 26,000 tanks, from 30,000 to 40,000 Armored Combat Vehicles (ACVs) and from 20,000 to 25,000 artillery guns. This is explained by the fact that seven Eastern European countries switched sides from the Warsaw Pact to NATO. If in 1990 NATO and the Soviet Union had approximately the same number of tanks and ACVs in Europe, in 2007 NATO enjoyed superiority by five to one.

3. There is a huge gap between the formal ceilings and actual holdings of five types of controlled weapons and military personnel. That difference was 8,000 tanks in 1999, when the CFE Treaty was adopted, and reached 11,000 tanks in 2007. So the treaty allows, instead of further reductions, to build up the number of tanks within the established ceilings by 50 percent. The gap for ACVs is 30 percent, for artillery 50 percent, and for combat aircraft and attack helicopters about 100 percent. Germany alone can build an additional 2,165 tanks, 877 ACVs, 1,075 artillery guns, 619 attack helicopters, and 91 combat airplanes. Germany can also increase the level of military personnel by 67 percent. Of course, this will never happen, but the option is on the table. The same is more or less true about other NATO members, except for Turkey and Greece, which fill their quotas by 80-90 percent, but for different reasons. The United States fills its quota by only 5-10 percent, since most of American regular forces have been deployed in Iraq and Afghanistan, and there are no plans to return them to Europe. Russia fills its CFE quotas of military personnel by only 40 percent; for tanks by 80 percent; for ACVs, by 87 percent; for artillery, by 93 percent; for combat aircraft by 52 percent; and for attack helicopters by 43 percent.

4. Since the ACFE Treaty abandoned the principle of bloc parity and establishing only national territorial limits, the ceilings for each member were established in a completely arbitrary manner. They do not correlate to any objective factors, such as the volume of gross domestic product (GDP), the length of borders, or the size of population. There is no rational to explain why Belarus has a ceiling of 1,800 tanks while France has a ceiling of 1,306 tanks, or why Italy has 1,348, and the United Kingdom (UK) has 1,015. Even

more confusing are the numbers for the actual holdings in 2007. For instance, Ukraine had 3,049 tanks and 4,250 ACVs, while Germany had only 1,904 tanks and 2404 ACVs, although German formal ceilings are much higher than the Ukrainian ones.

5. The restrictions on flank zones, which were retained in the ACFE Treaty, while all other zone ceilings were dropped, left Russia as practically the only country which is limited in deployment of forces in its own territory (technically, there are also some restrictions for the former Odessa military district in Ukraine and some eastern regions of Turkey). Under the ACFE Treaty, Russia's flank ceilings (Leningrad and Northern Caucasus military districts) were expanded from 700 to 1,300 tanks, from 580 to 2,140 ACVs, and from 1,280 to 1,680 artillery guns. But four NATO countries in the South (Turkey, Greece, Bulgaria, and Rumania) have combined ceilings of 7,380 tanks, 9,718 ACVs, and 8,368 artillery guns.

6. Another shortcoming of the CFE Treaty is that it counts only some of the weapons, which do not seem to reflect the real combat efficiency of modern weapons platforms. The recent wars demonstrated that the decisive role is performed by precision guidance weapons. About 90 percent of all the targets destroyed by air attacks in Kosovo, Afghanistan and Iraq were hit by American "smart" bombs and cruise missiles, while the impact of the "old" weapons was very limited. Thus, ironically, the CFE regime does not restrict the most important advanced military technology, capable of a surprise preemptive strike against a wide range of military and economic targets. It also does not restrict navies; although naval aircraft and ship launched cruise missiles (SLCMs) played a huge role in recent military conflicts.

7. Finally, the CFE Treaty hardly can perform as an all-European conventional arms control regime, since almost half of the European countries do not belong to it. The list of nonsignatories includes formal neutral states (Finland, Sweden, Switzerland, Austria, and Ireland), three Baltic states, and former republics of Yugoslavia. The military forces of these countries do not play a major role in the European balance. But practically all of them maintain partnership with NATO, and many participated in NATO-led peacekeeping operations (Bosnia, Kosovo, and Afghanistan). Although Estonia, Latvia, Lithuania, and Slovenia became NATO members in 2004, they did not join the CFE regime, following the Western position that links ratification of the ACFE Treaty to Russia's withdrawal from Moldova and Georgia.

MODERNIZATION OF THE CONVENTIONAL ARMS CONTROL REGIME

Despite all its shortcomings, the CFE should be preserved, which is possible only if its provisions are drastically modernized. A modernized conventional arms control regime in Europe is required to maintain and expand military transparency and equally to promote further reductions and downsizing of the Cold War conventional arsenals. The present crisis of the CFE Treaty requires bold and broad new initiatives. We need CFE-2 to ensure that a new unrestricted arms race is prevented, and national defense efforts are focused on new security challenges.

1. It makes sense to invite all European countries to join the new conventional arms control regiment. Since the CFE cannot be perceived as a West-East regime, all states, including Scandinavian and Balkan

countries, should be involved, as they are, for instance, involved on the Organization for Security and Co-operation in Europe (OSCE). Membership in a military alliance is no more a precondition for the participation in the CFE regime. This will help to strengthen European security in the Northern and Southern regions of the continent.

2. The CFE ceilings, adopted in 1999 in Istanbul should be replaced by new, much lower levels. As a first step, the CFE member-states should declare that they accept the levels of their actual holdings as a new ceiling, i.e., the actual numbers of military personnel and treaty limited weapons, and commit themselves not to exceed these levels in the future. Since the costs of weapons and military personnel skyrocketed in the last 2 decades, no member-state will be able (for budgetary reasons) to ever bridge the gap between the ACFE Treaty ceilings of 1999 and actual holdings of 2007. These commitments in practical terms will not require any country to abandon its weapons modernization programs, or transition from conscription-based to an all-volunteer armed force, but the proposed action will eliminate the gap between the permitted ceilings and actual holdings of weapons.

As a result, the ceilings for all member-states would immediately drop by 30-50 percent. These measures will not cost a penny, except the paper of a declaration, admitting the status quo. NATO will still maintain an impressive superiority of approximately 3:1 vs. Russia in all types of weapons and military personnel, although it will be a little bit smaller than under the terms of the ACFE Treaty.

3. The next step may require a declaration of intensions by member-states to further reduce the number of ground-based weapons (tanks, ACVs, and artillery)

by 20-25 percent within the next 10 years. Since almost all countries are in the middle of the retirement period of the weapons built during the Cold War and are beginning to replace them with a smaller number of more capable but very expensive weapon systems, the 20-25 percent reductions of holdings does not seem to be a radical departure from existing modernization plans. The commitment to reduce could be made easier by stipulations that some of the retired weapons may be stored or mothballed.

If this commitment is made, NATO, in Europe, will still maintain by the end of next decade, the largest concentration of military power in the world.

4. Another step should include immediate acceptance of the CFE Treaty by the new members of NATO: Baltic states and others. Since their actual holdings of heavy weapons are very small, their participation in the new regime, including the freeze and further reduction, will only help to advance European arms control.

5. NATO must agree to the elimination of the flank zones. It makes no sense to restrict freedom of deployment in sovereign territory for Russia, neither for Turkey or the Ukraine. It seems that technical solutions (raising the ceiling or reducing areas of the flank zones), are no more acceptable to Moscow. That is why the survival of the CFE will be impossible if the flank zones are not abandoned. But it is possible to suggest voluntarily a unilateral commitment to limit the forces in certain areas.

6. The most difficult step is related to plans to invite into NATO some former Soviet republics, in particular Ukraine and Georgia. Ukraine's CFE quota is quite impressive. After the dissolution of the USSR, Kiev acquired about 40 percent of the Soviet share of

the Treaty Limited Equipment (TLE). Today, Ukrainian ground forces are bigger than the ground forces of Germany. When former Soviet satellites joined NATO, they added a large number of weapons to NATO. Eastern European countries contributed more than a quarter of all ground weapons to NATO forces. If Ukraine is admitted to NATO, it will bring another 15 or 20 percent increase in NATO's levels. No doubt Moscow is taking a very negative view of Kiev's proposed membership in NATO. If the admission is given a green light, there will be no chance to save the CFE regime.

The proposed steps can help to revive the impetus for a conventional arms control regime in Europe, preserve and expand transparency, and prevent an unrestricted new arms race. A CFE-2 Treaty will also create better conditions for NATO-Russia security cooperation in a number of areas. The proposed steps do not resolve the problems of "smart" weapons and naval forces. But, they will help to provide new life for conventional arms control in the 21st century.

COOPERATION IN BMD

Russia is the only country which, for more than 30 years, has operated strategic BMD deployed around its capital. While some of these systems are outdated, Russia is developing a new generation of BMD systems. They included new modular radars and theater BMD interceptors S-400.

Russia strongly opposed the American plans for BMD deployment in Eastern Europe, claiming that they represent an element of the strategic BMD, which includes elements in Alaska and California, sea-based systems, and future space-based components. The Bush administration made it clear that the BMD deployment is an open-ended process and a further upgrade may follow. Moscow also considers BMD deployment in Eastern Europe a violation of the NATO Founding Act pledge to avoid "substantial" deployment on the territory of the new members of NATO.

The Russian proposal on cooperation with early warning in Gabala opens a window of opportunity to resolve the problem. While the old Gabala radar cannot be used for intercept purposes, the new Russian modular radar can, so access to the information collected by Russian radars helps to close the gap in existing American early warning systems. The information from Russian and American radars can be provided in real time to the Center for Information on Missile Launches, which Russia and the United States agreed to open in Moscow 11 years ago. For legal reasons, the Center has never been opened.

The cooperation in missile information collection can help to provide the data to battle management radars on American Aegis sea-based BMD systems deployed in the Eastern Mediterranean. Aegis interceptors and S-400 systems can provide protection against the missiles which Iran possesses today. These missile systems have a range of about 2,000 kilometers and can also be coordinated with the missile defenses developed by NATO. One should remember that under NATO-Russia auspices, experts have already prepared specific stipulations concerning joint theater BMDs.

While building joint BMD may be a very difficult task, it seems that coordinated deployment of Russian, American, and NATO BMDs with horizontal or vertical distribution of responsibilities is much more achievable. This cooperation can produce results much more quickly than unilateral American deployment in Eastern Europe, since the U.S. Congress denied the administration request for construction of the Ground Based Interceptor (GBI) base in Poland next year.

More importantly, the very fact of serious Russian, American, and NATO cooperation in BMD will send a powerful political message to Iran. It may help to reverse Iranian intentions to build nuclear weapons and long range missiles for their delivery.

AFGHANISTAN

Afghanistan is a crucial test. The NATO-led International Security Assistance Force (ISAF) has encountered many challenges in that country so far away from Europe. As a result, ISAF has not been very successful in destroying the Taliban and al-Qaeda.

The situation in Afghanistan may deteriorate even more when the United States recognizes its failure and begins to withdraw its forces. The shock wave of the defeat could be very serious. In any case, there is little chance to expect a quick victory in Afghanistan. At best, the task will be to maintain the status quo.

The situation in Afghanistan requires new efforts to maintain and expand the international coalition. Russia can become a major contributor to this effort. Moscow has important assets which can be very helpful to ISAF. Russia has ground and air military bases in Tajikistan and Kyrgyzstan, and many connections in Northern Afghanistan. While the Soviet experience in Afghanistan makes Russians unenthusiastic about new military involvement in that country, Russia clearly perceives the Taliban and al-Qaeda as her enemies.

Russia is also very much concerned about the drug traffic from Afghanistan. This problem has been greatly aggravated since the United States and NATO came to Afghanistan. Some Russians even accused the West of deliberately ignoring the drug problem and not taking action against the drug producers. Recently, this issue was recognized by ISAF, and some action has begun.

Probably Moscow might agree to accept greater responsibility for economic reconstruction of the northern provinces of Afghanistan.

Moscow ratified the Statute of Forces Agreement, which provides a legal framework for transition and presence of NATO personnel and materials on Russian territory. Russia concluded bilateral agreements with Germany, France, the United States, and some other countries on transit questions and permitted movement of NATO personnel and cargo to supply ISAF.

It seems that Afghanistan is a unique place where vital NATO and Russian security interests coincide. They face common enemies: Islamic terrorists and drug traffickers. It makes sense for Russia and the West to combine forces to deal with these threats.

The involvement of Russian security forces in Afghanistan could be very helpful for ISAF. But the problem of political control has to be resolved beforehand. One solution could be the NATO-Russia Council, which could provide a place for political decision-making.

If Russia and NATO agree to cooperate in Afghanistan, it could produce a real strategic partnership. Russia can contribute there much more than any prospective members of NATO. Besides, Russia can play a key role to help extend the anti-Taliban coalition, engaging China, India, and even Iran to help the fight against the common enemy.

All these steps can be made under the umbrella of the new All-European Security Pact, proposed by President Dmitry Medvedev, helping to create a security system from Vancouver, Canada, to Vladivostok, Russia.

It seems that there is a real window of opportunity for the North Atlantic Alliance and Russia to rethink their relationship—to institutionalize it with legally-binding agreements and a permanent decisionmaking mechanism so their common benefits would take priority over diverging interests.

ABOUT THE CONTRIBUTORS

STEPHEN J. BLANK has served as the Strategic Studies Institute's expert on the Soviet bloc and the post-Soviet world since 1989. Prior to that he was Associate Professor of Soviet Studies at the Center for Aerospace Doctrine, Research, and Education, Maxwell Air Force Base, Alabama; and taught at the University of Texas, San Antonio; and at the University of California, Riverside. Dr. Blank is the editor of *Imperial Decline: Russia's Changing Position in Asia*, coeditor of *Soviet Military and the Future*, and author of *The Sorcerer as Apprentice: Stalin's Commissariat of Nationalities, 1917-1924*. He has also written many articles and conference papers on Russia, the Commonwealth of Independent States, and Eastern European security issues. Dr. Blank's current research deals with proliferation and the revolution in military affairs, and energy and security in Eurasia. His two most recent books are *Russo-Chinese Energy Relations: Politics in Command*, (London, UK: Global Markets Briefing, 2006); and *Natural Allies? Regional Security in Asia and Prospects for Indo-American Strategic Cooperation* (Carlisle, PA: Strategic Studies Institute, U.S. Army War College, 2005). Dr. Blank holds a B.A. in history from the University of Pennsylvania, and an M.A. and Ph.D. in history from the University of Chicago.

LOUIS H. JORDAN, JR., is the Deputy Director of the Strategic Studies Institute, U.S. Army War College, Carlisle, PA. He is a colonel in the U.S. Army. He recently returned from a deployment to Afghanistan where he served as Senior Military Advisor to the Afghan Deputy Minister of Interior for Counter Narcotics. Colonel Jordan has served in aviation assignments from company through brigade and the national level including service at the National Guard Bureau as an operations officer, branch chief, and as the Deputy Division Chief of the Aviation and Safety Division. Colonel Jordan has commanded at the battalion, brigade, and joint task force level to include command of Joint Task Force Raven, the aviation task force for Operation JUMP START along the Southwest Border in Arizona. Colonel Jordan holds a B.A. in sociology from Fordham University in the Bronx, NY; a master's degree in strategic studies from the U.S. Army War College, and a certification in strategic planning from the American Management Association.

JEFFREY D. MCCAUSLAND is Visiting Professor of International Security at Dickinson College. He also holds the position of Distinguished Visiting Professor of Research and Minerva Chair at the Strategic Studies Institute (SSI), U.S. Army War College. A U.S. Army colonel (retired), during his military career he served in a variety of command and staff positions in the United States and Europe. This included assignments as the Dean of Academics at the U.S. Army War College, Carlisle Barracks, PA, and the Office of the Deputy Chief of Staff for Operations, working on the Conventional Forces in Europe Treaty (CFE) from 1988 to 1989. He commanded the 3rd Battalion 17th Field Artillery, VII Corps during Operations DESERT SHIELD and DESERT STORM. Dr. McCausland was also the Director for Defense Policy and Arms Control on the National Security Council Staff in the White House. Furthermore, he was a member of the Department of Social Sciences, U.S. Military Academy, West Point, NY; a visiting fellow at the Center for International Affairs, Harvard University; and a research fellow at the International Institute for Strategic Studies, London. Dr. McCausland's articles have appeared in *The*

Fletcher Forum, Parameters, Naval War College Review, Comparative Strategy, Armed Forces and Society, Defense Analysis, Field Artillery Journal, Military Review, and *International Defense Review*. He is also the author of *The Gulf War: A Military Analysis* (International Institute for Strategic Studies, London). He is a contributing author or editor to a number of books, including *The Future of the Special Relationships, Conventional Deterrence, The Future of US-Australian Relations*, and *Arms Control in the 1990s*. Dr. McCausland holds a Ph.D. in international relations from the Fletcher School of Law and Diplomacy, Tufts University.

SERGEY ROGOV is Director of the Institute for the U.S. and Canadian Studies. He previously held a number of positions at the Institute of USA and Canada including: Junior Research Fellow and Senior Research Fellow of the Department of Foreign Policy, Chief of a Section and later Chief of the Department of Military and Political Studies, Representative of the Institute in the Soviet Embassy in the United States, Leading Research Fellow, and Deputy Director. Dr. Rogov is the author of 300 articles and 16 books, including "The Role of the National Security Advisor in the US Decision-Making Process"; "The Search for a Balance of Interests in the Soviet-American Relations"; "The USSR and the USA: Problems of Mutual Security"; "The Evolving Military Doctrine of Russia"; "Russian Foreign Policy: Three Years of Trial and Error"; *The Eurasian Strategy for Russia; The Russian Financial Crash of 1998; Nuclear Weapons in the Multipolar World; The New Stage in Russian-American Relations;* and "Russia in the New International System." Dr. Rogov holds the Candidate degree in historical sciences and a Doctorate in historical sciences in 1984 from the Institute of USA and Canada.

PAUL SCHULTE is a nonresident senior associate in the Carnegie Nuclear Policy Program and at Carnegie Europe, where his research focuses on the future of deterrence, nuclear strategy, nuclear nonproliferation, cyber security, and their political implications. He is a senior visiting fellow in the Disarmament and Globalization Program at the University of London's School of Oriental and African Studies. Additionally, he is a senior visiting fellow at both the Centre for Defense Studies at King's College at the University of London and the Centre for the Study of Global Governance at the London School of Economics and Political Science. Mr. Shulte previously served as chief speechwriter to two United Kingdom (UK) defense secretaries (2006–07), as director of proliferation and arms control for the UK Ministry of Defence, and as UK commissioner on the United Nations (UN) commissions for Iraqi disarmament, United Nations Special Commission (UNSCOM) and United Nations Monitoring, Verification and Inspection Commission (UNMOVIC) (1997–2002). He also worked in Iraq's Coalition Provisional Authority as director of defense organization in the Office of National Security Affairs (2004), the office responsible for rebuilding the Iraqi Ministry of Defense, and was founding head of the UK Post Conflict Reconstruction Unit (2004–05) involved in planning the initial integrated British civil-military campaign in Helmand province in Afghanistan. Mr. Shulte holds a B.Sc. in economics from the London School of Economics; and a Professional Certification in Group Analysis, London Centre for Psychotherapy. He is a graduate of the Senior Officers Course, Royal College of Defense Studies; and an International Fellow, Weatherhead Center for International Affairs, Harvard University.